# ADVANCE PRAISE

*"Innovative and enterprising, AdmitHub is championing the adoption of artificial intelligence to provide better student services in higher education!"*

—CLARK V. BRIGGER, ASSISTANT VICE PRESIDENT FOR UNDERGRADUATE EDUCATION AND EXECUTIVE DIRECTOR FOR UNDERGRADUATE ADMISSIONS, PENNSYLVANIA STATE UNIVERSITY

*"The means of communication in today's world are more robust than ever, yet reaching our students is more challenging than ever. AdmitHub understands how students communicate, and their cutting-edge technology and innovative thinking will undoubtedly cause us all to rethink how we communicate with our students."*

—MIKE KNOX, VICE PRESIDENT FOR STUDENT AFFAIRS, WEST TEXAS A&M UNIVERSITY

*"Enrollment managers and admissions staff are always at least half a generation removed from the students they're working with (and oftentimes, more). Keeping up with changing trends and preferences among the new recruits is always a challenge, but Kirk Daulerio's work provides valuable insight for anyone in the profession."*

—JON BOECKENSTEDT, ASSOCIATE VICE PRESIDENT, ENROLLMENT MANAGEMENT AND MARKETING, DEPAUL UNIVERSITY

*"AdmitHub allows universities to deliver a personalized student journey by what I refer to as "automating with personality." I believe the technology they are developing will become essential for universities to thrive as more Generation Z students navigate their way into higher education."*

—BREANNA EDWARDS, DIRECTOR OF STUDENT LIFE, UNIVERSITY OF THE WEST OF SCOTLAND

*"With texting being today's preferred communication medium, AdmitHub's leading-edge service has been greatly instrumental in optimizing our connectivity to prospective students throughout the enrollment funnel."*

—CORNELL LESANE, VICE PRESIDENT FOR ENROLLMENT AND DEAN OF ADMISSIONS, ALLEGHENY COLLEGE

*"If you are an admission professional looking for an in-depth look at how best to engage with Generation Z as part of the college selection process, you should look no further than this book. Daulerio and his AdmitHub team are on the cutting edge of how best to reach this next generation of applicants. This should be required reading for every VP of Enrollment looking to improve their enrollment communication plan."*

—ERIC NICHOLS, VICE PRESIDENT FOR ENROLLMENT
AND DEAN OF ADMISSION, SAINT ANSELM COLLEGE

*"AdmitHub is the undisputed leader in connecting with today's tech-savvy college-bound students and provides educators with the time and flexibility to focus on their most pressing issues."*

—DANIEL BLEDNICK, DIRECTOR OF COLLEGE
GUIDANCE, THE TEAK FELLOWSHIP

# ENGAGING GENERATION Z

# ENGAGING GENERATION Z

## SUPPORTING COLLEGE-BOUND STUDENTS WITH INTELLIGENT MOBILE MESSAGING

## KIRK DAULERIO
### ADRIAN SERNA

ENGAGING GENERATION Z

*Supporting College-Bound Students*
*with Intelligent Mobile Messaging*

ISBN   978-1-5445-0047-8  *Paperback*

　　　　978-1-5445-0048-5  *Ebook*

# CONTENTS

# INTRODUCTION

*When I was ten years old*
*I remember thinking how cool it would be*
*When we were going on an eight-hour drive*
*If I could just watch TV.*

—BRAD PAISLEY, *WELCOME TO THE FUTURE*

College application time. I remember sitting in my northeast Philadelphia basement, banging out pithy text on a clunky typewriter in hopes of catching the attention of some intimidating admission officer at a college far, far away. As a first-generation college student, I was bursting with questions: Am I good enough? Should I study engineering because I'm strong in math? What are the students like at this college? How do I know if my family can afford it?

Most of the answers—and even the right questions—remained unknown. I sought the advice of people around me—my counselor, a few teachers, my parents, and friends—but they knew only so much and couldn't offer the specific assistance I needed.

After college, I found myself on the other side of the table—as a professional in the world of college admission. I chose that career direction for the same reason many people do: to help shepherd young people toward this transformational opportunity.

The core of my work was always connecting with students. The way our admission team communicated with students ten or fifteen years ago was much simpler: we sent out brochures in the mail, visited high schools to speak about the virtues of our institution, invited students for campus visits and interviews, and contacted students by phone if they showed interest. We competed with peer institutions for students but not to the degree to which we are seeing in today's hyperconnected environment.

E-mail came along in the mid-1990s, and communications—as well as the competition among colleges for students—kicked up a notch. Bam! In the early years, e-mails were personalized. We in the admission profession had the time and inclination to connect with students through this easy new medium. I even remember the mini thrill every time the "You've got mail!" notification popped up on my computer between rounds of MacGolf (boy, do I miss that game).

These days, however, there is simply too much noise in this process. E-mail automation has created an enormous volume of spam. This, combined with the challenge of sifting through an overload of information on the Internet, makes it hard for students to find answers. **Students are tuning out, even though they still desperately need help navigating the college road map.**

Where are students in Generation Z most engaged? On their mobile devices, of course. But not so much to read and respond to e-mail and hardly for talking. My teenage children don't even have their voice mail set up. Not surprisingly, Generation Z interacts via social media and, of course, messaging.

Only 20 percent of e-mails sent to Generation Z are opened, but **98 percent of text messages are read within fifteen minutes.** There's a lesson—and opportunity—in this for the education profession. Texting is a platform that can provide students the support they need in a personalized way. To keep up with their constituency—that is, students—colleges need a communications strategy that is as nimble as its Gen Z target.

College can be the turning point in the lives of many young adults. We want them to succeed, but we also know they face many challenges. Some 14 percent of students intending to enroll never actually show up on campus for their first year, and nearly half of students enrolled don't make it to graduation.

Education professionals empathize with students and their struggles. If you're like me, student success is what drives you. You want to hear about the master's degree candidate who is the first person in his family to even attend college. Or the once-homeless kid who stuck to her dream of a university education. Or the student who remained in the game—and excelled—when it would have been so easy to call it quits. But there are also days when your job feels less like connecting students with their dreams and more like an endless set of administrative drudgeries and an overflowing in-box.

While every dedicated professional cares deeply about his or her students, tools like e-mail and mailers are difficult to scale in a personalized way. Sure, we can add a name to our note, but mail merge doesn't truly allow for personal connections.

This sense that it's impossible to build a personal relationship with each student is understandable. However, it's not inevitable. Technology opens once-never-envisioned possibilities for universities across the country, indeed, around the world.

The simple solution lies in **mobile messaging powered by artificial intelligence.** Imagine having thousands of individual conversations simultaneously while still feeling that impactful interaction you get during a thirty-minute phone call with a student. The end results match: you are able to answer questions and put the student at ease. And even more, what if you could efficiently and effectively provide gentle nudges **when a student needed them, to act proactively rather than reactively?** You could abandon the uncomfortable (and often unproductive) role of e-mail spammer. No more flooding e-mail in-boxes, forcing students to wait, or driving students away.

I've worked with dozens of enrollment leaders who've wished there were "a hundred more of me" just to be able to respond to students in a timely fashion. Admission offices get the same questions year after year: What's the early application deadline? What's the average SAT score for accepted students? From whom do I have to get letters of recommendation? When is the Free Application for Federal Student Aid (FAFSA) deadline? What vaccinations do I need? Are all the freshmen dorms co-ed? When will I know who my roommate is?

The answers don't change much from year to year, but the expectations do. Students want fast responses; they are used to real-time interactions. Admission offices, as well as other services throughout our institutions, want to show students that they value them. Universities want customized engagement that builds community, both today and tomorrow when those students become alumni. And frankly, universities, just like businesses and government agencies, are judged by their technology.

Never before have we been able to make such a meaningful, personalized connection with so many students. With technology, you can maintain an ongoing conversation that supports each and every student, from the time they first show interest in your institution until they walk across that stage with a diploma in hand.

This technology can help students achieve their educational aspirations and help enrollment officers and other university officials have more fulfilling career experiences. You'll not only connect with students, but you'll also go beyond to **reconnect with why you entered the profession in the first place.**

Technology, once again, has sparked a paradigm shift, rewriting the way we support students within the education process. Once upon a time, we sent handwritten letters via Pony Express, knowing it would take weeks for a response. Today, we look at a screen in our hand and see and talk directly to someone we love.

In this book, readers will gain:

1. A thorough understanding of Generation Z and its expectations for communication
2. Knowledge of communication methods that meet those expectations
3. Clarity on how messaging capitalizes on those methods
4. Insight into how artificial intelligence can supercharge your staff and scale student support

## HOW TO READ THIS BOOK

Our hope is that this book will serve as an invaluable guide as readers develop their monthly, quarterly, and annual communication strategies. We also designed it as a reference that readers can return to when they need to address immediate needs. For quick reference, the beginning of each chapter lists Key Takeaways that summarize the most salient points in each chapter.

If you're new to college admission, taking time to digest the entire book will help you establish a solid understanding of the current landscape for recruiting across the United States. If you've been in the college admission industry for a while, chapter 1 won't present any new information. Read it as a refresher or skip directly to chapter 2 to learn more about your newest crop of students, Generation Z. Continue reading from there to gain insight into how to adapt your outreach to meet these students' expectations.

Although designed for professionals in education, the lessons in this book extend beyond academia. For example, if you're interested in relationship management, there is guidance and information within these pages to help you modernize your methods and hone your communication technique. Chapters 2, 3, 5, and 6 are especially salient.

The information in this book may come via the lens of the college application and enrollment process, but the crux is how ongoing conversational support can help change behavior to foster success. The ideas and principles are applicable to any industry dealing with a large audience of young people: nonprofit organizations, high school districts, teachers and professors, and so on.

Welcome to the future.

# Terms

### AI
when a machine mimics "cognitive" functions

### MACHINE LEARNING
ability to "learn" without explicit programming

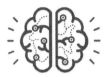

### AI ASSISTANT
a bot that performs tasks or services for an individual

### CHATBOT
a bot that uses human language to communicate

### NLP/NLU/NLG
interaction between computers and humans using natural languages

# EVOLUTION OF COLLEGE COMMUNICATIONS

**KEY TAKEAWAYS**

- Student recruitment efforts have multiplied across various channels in the past several decades, but enrollment staff size has remained fairly constant, leaving leaders feeling unable to support every student effectively.
- Traditional methods of reaching students—among them campus visits, direct mail, phone calls, e-mail, and social media—remain valuable, but they present logistical challenges for enrollment teams aiming to provide personalized student support.

- With so much information available to students 24-7, Gen Z is conditioned to put up its blinders to information it feels is not **timely or relevant.**
- Mobile messaging has become the best way to capture students' attention and provide them with personalized assistance.

Every year, more than two million teenagers decide to go to college. While students and their families tour campuses across the country, wade through university-branded materials, and stress over the final decision, college admission officers, too, are under pressure. To attract and retain the best and the brightest, to fill their campuses with a rich diversity of students—the citizen leaders of tomorrow—they must be able to reach those potential students and roll out the welcome mat. It can be a complex challenge that sometimes pushes admission staff to their max.

Every professional facing this challenge is on the hunt for tools and communication channels that are efficient, effective, and customized to meet the distinct characteristics of the latest generation of college goers. Oh, yes, and it all has to fit within the budget.

The fall 2015 edition of the Admission Benchmarking Study (ABS) published by the North American Coalition for Christian Admission Professionals (NACCAP) reported some noteworthy statistics on college recruiting costs.[1] In 2015, the overall cost for a college to recruit a single student was $3,214. This was a 6.6 percent jump from $3,015 in 2014. Not surprisingly, the data show a steady and significant increase over the past several decades. In fact, in 1993 the price tag on recruiting a student was only $1,414. To attract one student to campus today is **over 127 percent more expensive** than it was then.

You might assume inflation is to blame, but the Department of Labor's Consumer Price Index (CPI) Inflation Calculator shows that inflation explains only about half the increase.

The ABS also found that as recruitment ramped up, college enrollment leaders felt understaffed given the level of service needed to provide every student with the support necessary to successfully navigate application and enrollment.

## CAMPUS VISITS AND INFORMATION SESSIONS

The campus visit and information session stands as the crown jewel of college admission recruitment, and for

---

1    https://s3.amazonaws.com/credo-naccap/reports/2015+NACCAP+Admission+Benchm arking+Study+-+Summary+Report.pdf

good reason. It's the perfect way for a college to show off its virtues, to generate buzz and excitement, and to make a personal connection with every student. How many tour guides have uttered, "If you like us on a rainy day like today, you'll love us the rest of the year"?

Campus visits are not only important to colleges; they are also important to students and their families. The *Boston Globe* reported in 2015 that colleges across the United States were seeing large increases in the number of campus visitors.[2] Harvard University expected forty thousand campus visitors that season, more than twice the number from a decade ago. In 2014, more than seventy thousand visitors attended tours and information sessions at Boston University, up 33 percent from the previous year.

An upswing in visitors presents logistical challenges for admission staff, who recognize the campus visit as a one-and-done phenomenon. Students may have a wonderful experience on campus talking with admission staff, tour guides, and even faculty, but how does a college maintain the connection once the students have headed off to the next college on the list?

Second, how does the admission staff make a "personal"

---

2   https://www.bostonglobe.com/lifestyle/style/2015/06/10/bananas-campus-deal-breaker/n5YIoM2uO9qvRz9aCiV1dP/story.html

link so that students don't reject a school based on superficial criteria? The *Boston Globe* article found students citing a host of reasons for opting out of schools. One student scratched a college from her list because her flight from the East Coast to California was too long. Similarly, cafeteria food, campus architecture, and the campus "vibe" can be enough to tip the pro-con balance. All that said, however, students are most positively influenced when they feel some level of personal connection during campus visits.

## DIRECT MAIL

During my tenure as a college admission officer, the tried-and-true college brochure was our tool of choice. I remember the painstaking hours it took to review, revise, and creatively design the many publications we mailed to different groups of students around the country and the world.

Direct mail puts vibrant, informative advertising in the hands of prospective students and their families. Colleges want dinner conversations to include comments such as, "Isn't that a pretty quad, Darlene?"

On the flip side, printed brochures are easily disposable, expensive, prone to noise, and without guarantee that the intended student will ever read the information. To underscore that point, a friend whose child is a rising high school senior sent me this photo of his dining room table:

Perhaps most importantly, print mail is a one-sided communication that heavily taxes the resources of admission and enrollment team members. There's zero opportunity for back-and-forth engagement unless a student takes the initiative to read the brochure and then visit the college's website to fill out an inquiry form or pick up the phone and call the admission office.

While studies suggest that people play close attention to printed material—it's a lasting, tangible reminder of a college's interest—digital communication is becoming the best way to capture the current generation of college-bound students. Ruffalo Noel Levitz noted in its

*2015 E-Expectations Report* that 60 percent of high school seniors are more likely to consider institutions that use e-mail, text messaging, and social media to communicate with them.[3]

## PHONE CALLS

A one-to-one conversation between a college admission officer and a student is, obviously, the best way to establish a personal relationship and generate excitement about the institution. Phoning students, especially when they are interested in the school but cannot visit, seems an ideal way to keep the conversation going throughout the college application process. It stands to reason that because Gen Zers are so connected to their phones that they'd welcome the opportunity to talk, right?

Wrong. Gen Z uses the phone for text messaging or social media, not talking. Nine times out of ten, unsolicited calls are sent directly to voice mail—if the students even have voice mail set up!

---

3   https://omniupdate.com/_resources/pdfs/research/2015_eexpectations.pdf

Bob Bardwell, who directs counseling at Monson Innovation High School in Monson, Massachusetts, says his students "often ignore phone calls if they don't know who is calling" or if the caller ID indicates a random university. "Only if they are very interested in the school do they typically show an interest in the phone calls," he adds, defining "very interested" as having sent a deposit. "They especially get annoyed when they get multiple phone calls in short periods of time during the 'recruitment' process."

Bardwell encourages his students to call colleges about individual issues but finds they are "so scared" to do so.

"They are not used to talking to strangers, and even some of my most capable students are petrified by the thought of having to speak to someone they don't know," he says. "They often want me to do it for them, ask what to say, and get very nervous."

Ruffalo Noel Levitz reported that only 13 percent of high school seniors and 7 percent of juniors found answers to their questions about a college over the phone. That means the vast majority of phone calls in the college recruiting process are college initiated, unless it's a call to the financial aid office about the tuition bill.

The bottom line is that while direct conversation is crucial in supporting students through the enrollment process, phone calls are minimally effective.

## E-MAIL

You may remember e-mail starting out slowly and on a limited, individual basis. Back in the early days, the only people who sent you e-mails were people you knew. Such a novel idea today when, for every personalized e-mail you receive, you're spammed with a dozen or more marketing ads and e-mail campaigns. It's no wonder that students (and everyone else) are tuning out e-mails. **The open rates for e-mail today hover around 20 percent.**

Still, e-mail is an effective way for colleges to message students at scale and provide important information about their institutions. *Higher Education Marketing* published a blog post in 2015 that offered helpful tips for messaging students:[4]

- Stop sending e-mail blasts; instead, personalize and provide relevant content
- Be sure to follow permission requirements—single opt-in is good, but double-opt-in is even better
- Use an e-mail service provider to manage targeted campaigns
- Simplify and inform in subject lines and avoid being "salesy"
- Make certain the preview filter (the copy and image people see before they open an e-mail) is relevant
- Time of day and day of week are important considerations when sending e-mail campaigns

Colleges put a great deal of time and effort into their e-mail communications in hopes that students will open the e-mails, browse the senders' websites, and complete the inquiry forms and applications.

---

4    http://www.higher-education-marketing.com/
     blog/10-quick-tips-improve-student-recruitment-email-campaigns

## SOCIAL MEDIA

Social media, perhaps not surprisingly, has become a primary way to engage with the world. Glance around the next time you're in a grocery store, in a mall, or even walking down the street. Almost everyone is staring at their phones. Odds are, they're on social media. And why not? There's so much to do and see on social media, with the added benefit that the reward receptor in the brain is activated every time someone likes or shares your post.

The universality of social media is staggering. Hootsuite recently shared figures gleaned from surveys administered by Harris Poll and We Are Social:[5]

- At the end of 2016, 2.8 billion people were connected to social media
- 83 percent of Americans have a social media account (in the United Kingdom, it's 77 percent)
- Facebook has more than a billion daily active users (989 million on mobile)
- 6,000 tweets are sent every second
- Instagram is one of the five most-used apps, and more than 40 billion (and counting) photos have been shared

---

5   https://blog.hootsuite.com/social-media-in-higher-education/

Social media allows colleges to get information in front of students where they are, without making them search for it on a website. But social media—ever changing and fleeting—are primarily one-way communications tools. How does this affect social media strategies directed at Gen Z?

With so much information buzzing on their mobile devices at all times, Gen Zers are conditioned to put up their blinders to information that is not **timely or relevant** to them. Their attention spans are shorter than those of the previous generation, and when they focus on a topic, near-instant gratification is expected.[6]

Students tend to be the earliest adopters of new technology, which means that the technology used to communicate with them must be nimble, otherwise it quickly becomes obsolete. College admission teams must continually shift their marketing methods to meet students where they spend their time.

So what's the best way to get relevant, personalized information to Gen Z while satisfying its desire for immediate feedback?

---

6    https://www.slideshare.net/sparksandhoney/generation-z-final-june-17/

## MESSAGING

The way in which people communicate, even digitally, is best described as **conversation**. For that reason, the style and length of e-communication have shifted toward shorter, back-and-forth messages.

For Generation Z, that translates into text messaging and online chat. As of 2015, **the top four messaging apps had more downloads, greater usage, and longer retention rates than the top four social networks.**[7] The demographics are wide among chat app users, most of whom are high school and college aged.

Ruffalo Noel Levitz points to a huge gap between high schoolers' welcoming attitude toward messaging from colleges and the number of colleges that message prospective students on a mass scale. In the *2015 E-Expectations Report*,[8] **73 percent of high school seniors would welcome a text message from colleges, yet only 29 percent receive one.** To create a more seamless path to enrollment and graduate success, mobile messaging should be integrated into the student communication flow.

In addition to text messaging, many colleges use messag-

---

7   http://www.businessinsider.com/the-messaging-app-report-2016-4-23

8   https://www.ruffalonl.com/
    papers-research-higher-education-fundraising/2015/2015-e-expectations-report

ing apps such as WeChat and WhatsApp to communicate with international students. We're also seeing colleges get more comfortable with the most popular messaging apps such as Facebook Messenger and Snapchat. How are your puppy filter skills?

Of all the methods of communication used with students, colleges see the highest response rate from mobile messaging. The **average reply rate for text messaging is 40 percent,**[9] so it's important to ensure that staff members are equipped to handle responses in an efficient and timely manner. (In chapter 5, we discuss how a college's already-overstretched staff can manage all these simultaneous conversations.)

Let's take a deeper dive into the mindset of Generation Z: who are they, what makes them tick, and what they expect from you.

---

9   https://martech.zone/text-messaging/

# (2)

# GENERATION Z

**KEY TAKEAWAYS**

- Generation Z, which accounts for 25 percent of the US population, has never lived in a world without the Internet.
- Being born into the age of the Internet means having the ability to engage in a global conversation with anyone and everyone at the touch of a button.
- With instant access to information, movies, and music through most devices, Gen Z has been groomed for an on-demand lifestyle. In short, Gen Z doesn't like to wait.
- Information tailored to reach Gen Zers must be customized, conversational, and mobile optimized, or you risk losing them.

For readers familiar with the evolution of college communication to students and who may have breezed through chapter 1, essentially colleges are utilizing a variety of methods to engage prospective students, but the key to unlocking meaningful connections with them is through two-way mobile messaging. The reason for this shift lies with the newest generation of students, Generation Z.

## WHO IS GENERATION Z?

Just as we were getting used to all of the talk about Millennials, another generation emerges: Generation Z. These young Americans have thrust themselves into the spotlight like a new Snapchat filter, Unicorn Frappuccino, or music festival.

They are the the country's most technologically reliant—and savvy—generation. They elevate multitasking to a new level. There are also indications that they are more realistic and less idealistic than their parents and that they are geared toward entrepreneurial thinking. They are coming of age at a time marked by economic and political turmoil, so their life view is more guarded. They are socially progressive.

Generation Z has also been called Gen I or iGen because, born in the mid-1990s, its members have **never lived in**

**a world without the Internet.** The Internet has been so ubiquitous in their lives that most don't even remember when we used to call it the World Wide Web and URLs started with "www."

Gen Zers are the offspring of Generation Xers (hence the nomenclature) and some Millennials. They are one of the fastest-growing demographics with more than seventy million people.[10] One of every four people in the United States is a Gen Zer.[11] Being born into a connected world

---

10  http://www.theatlantic.com/sponsored/goldman-sachs-2016/
what-if-i-told-you-gen-z-matters-more-than-millennials/903/

11  https://www.forbes.com/sites/thehartmangroup/2016/03/31/
new-kids-on-the-block-a-first-look-at-gen-z/#529e3e891bab

has shaped many of the characteristics of this generation that now accounts for more than a quarter of the US population.[12] This chapter explores how they differ from their counterparts of the past, including their desire for on-demand information, rapid consumption of parcels of info, untethered connectivity, and modern conversational style.

## DIFFERENT FROM PAST GENERATIONS

The implications for always existing in a world with the Internet are sweeping. Think about it in the context of a shoemaker we'll call Miguel. His clients are those he's able to connect with on a regular basis. There would have been a time, say Pre-Industrial Revolution, when Miguel's customers would be his friends, family, and the people in his town who, when they needed shoes, stopped by his shop to order a pair. By comparison, if he lived after the Industrial Revolution, Miguel would own a few sewing machines, word would spread about his shoes through a local newspaper article written by a satisfied client, and people would phone in their orders. Miguel would have clients from all the neighboring cities and a few from across the state.

---

12  https://www.forbes.com/sites/thehartmangroup/2016/03/31/
new-kids-on-the-block-a-first-look-at-gen-z/#529e3e891bab

Now imagine he lives in the age of the Internet. A national magazine publishes a feature story about Miguel's artisan shoes, and he has to hire administrators for customer service, human resources, and operations just to keep up. Let's say Miguel is launching his organic, ethically sourced, energy-neutral, side hustle-turned-main hustle shoemaking business to a Generation Z customer base. He posts pictures of some of his creations on Instagram, replies to reviews on Yelp, and is ranked on a Buzzfeed list of "10 Shoes You #NeedRightNow."

Miguel connects with millions of potential customers (aka followers) who span the globe and simply must have his shoes. Because each of those followers wants to feel connected and heard, his staff includes a social media manager who handles the hundreds of questions, mentions, retweets, and "likes" that come in daily.

Being born into the age of the Internet means Gen Zers have the ability to engage in a global conversation with anyone and everyone at the touch of a button. The Brand Team for Consumer Apps at Google reports on the importance of the conversation between Gen Z and institutions. The brands that Gen Zers connect with and hold in the highest regard are representations of their values and their expectations of themselves and their peers.[13]

---

13   https://storage.googleapis.com/think/docs/its-lit.pdf

To position itself for success, every college and university should, essentially, look at itself as a brand seeking to connect with this new generation. For enrollment, this means branding the in-person experience in a way that sets it apart from other academic institutions. To win Gen Z, it also means branding the college in a way that goes beyond its physical campus to include its values and mission.

### EVERYTHING ON-DEMAND

Every previous generation experienced a time without broadband Internet. Baby boomers typed words directly onto paper or waited by the mailbox for a letter from a pen pal. Generation X grew accustomed to using computers and learned how they could reduce the physical space needed for data. They patiently booted up their computers and loaded Oregon Trail through command prompts.

As technology advanced exponentially, Millennials tuned out the shrieks and beeps associated with getting online. They didn't mind the top-down incremental image loading; they remembered waiting all night to download a single MP3 of their favorite song. Gen Z's predecessors raised the bar for technological speed, so Gen Zers now inhabit a world where they can watch their favorite TV shows on devices in their hands, listen to any song they desire anywhere, anytime, and look at loved ones while they talk to them hundreds or even thousands of miles away.

Theirs is a world that doesn't think, "Wow, that was fast." Rather, it questions, "Why is that so slow?" Gen Zers are so immersed in speedy technology that they're referred to as digital natives.[14] In short, while every previous generation was conditioned to "wait," Gen Z desires **instant gratification.**

Immediate access to information, movies, and music through most devices has groomed Gen Zers for an on-demand lifestyle. When they have a question, they get the answer with a few clicks, swipes, or voice commands. To learn about Ancient Greece, they may never locate an encyclopedia, pick up the correct volume, and flip through the pages until they land on the article they need. Instead, they will type into a search engine or maybe even ask Siri or Alexa. They still need to understand how to properly vet a source or answer, but one fact remains: **they get answers, instantly.**

Gen Z's quick Q&A-style investigating extends beyond academic-oriented research to almost any aspect of life. Like a curious toddler asking his mother "Why?" rapid-

---

14  http://www.tig.co.uk/blogs/generation-z-the-digital-natives/

fire Gen Z can get answers to even mundane questions such as "How much sleep do I need?" "When is Mother's Day?" or "What noise do squirrels make?"

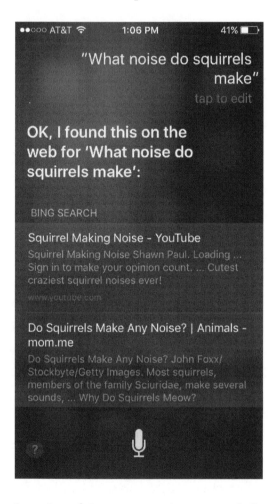

Technology doesn't just connect Gen Zers to *information* in real time but also to *people* in real time. Consider a father running errands and texting to check in on the tween he dropped off at the mall:

Because they are able to send quick pieces of conversation and ask questions over a text, Gen Zers bypass the process of making a phone call, leaving a voice mail, and waiting for a callback. These young people have integrated this circumvention into other parts of life. Students text classmates to find out the homework when their teacher is slow to update his web portal, they use a group text to organize the work on a project, and they even get nervous when a crush doesn't text back quickly enough.

What's important to focus on is that **Gen Z doesn't like to wait.**

## "BYTE"-SIZED CONSUMPTION

In tandem with getting information on demand, this generation operates with an adapted attention span. Digital "snacking" is how Generation Z consumes. According to Sparks & Honey, the average Gen Z attention span has decreased from twelve seconds (as recorded in 2000) to eight seconds.[15] This means multiparagraph e-mails, hour-long lectures, and phone calls no longer have the same impact they once did on youth. While not necessarily a bad thing, this creates a challenge in grabbing and holding their attention.

Gen Z is also more nimble at processing different types of information quickly. It can easily jump from watching a Netflix movie on TV, to editing an essay on a school

15  https://www.slideshare.net/sparksandhoney/generation-z-final-june-17

computer, to checking a text message on a phone, to posting on Instagram on a tablet, to adding their portion of Google Slides presentation on a personal laptop. They do all of this seamlessly, even with multiple distractions in the background.[16]

As older generations shift to accommodate this abbreviated attention span, so does the media. Consider how differently information is packaged today. Like those small chunks of conversation in every text message, information is now more "snack" size. News is updated in tweets of 140 characters instead of in multiparagraph articles. Sites such as BuzzFeed tell stories with image-laden slides. And virtually every media source now embeds online videos to engage audiences. There's been a migration away from the notion that people will automatically consume information because it's available. Instead, the information must be engaging and crafted to fit a generation always ready to head on to the next thing.

## UNTETHERED AND ALWAYS CONNECTED

Smartphones are the tool of choice for Gen Zers, who use them to access the Internet. They spend more time connected than not.[17] "Always on," they have the oppor-

16   http://www.huffingtonpost.com/george-beall/8-key-differences-between_b_12814200.html

17   http://www.turner.com/pressroom/turner-research-shares-key-insights-plurals-and-millennials%E2%80%99-media-consumption-and

tunity to connect with the world from anywhere—and be reached from anywhere. Smartphones keep them in the loop when a friend tags them in a Facebook post, Instagram lets them know when a follower likes one of their pictures, ESPN sends them an update when their team scores, and iMessage notifies them when they receive a new message.

Gen Z **passively consumes** information—in all its different forms—instead of actively seeking it out. This distinction places more responsibility on media creators such as entertainers, news sources, and even educators who seek to **actively engage** members of Gen Z.

While information has shifted to reach Gen Zers wherever they are, the graphical representation has also adapted. Companies and institutions are abandoning sites with Flash, thin fonts, and an abundance of images, replacing them with sites with HTML5, bolder typefaces, and single images that easily scale for mobile viewing.

Gen Z has embraced the small screen and mobile user interface where hidden functions appear with a click or swipe, and functions are represented with an icon instead of words. In fact, they've become so detached from the origin of some icons that they don't know what they actually represent. If you want a laugh, just ask a Gen Zer what the Save icon is.

Entire industries have adapted to the always-connected lifestyle. During a focus group of students ages seventeen to nineteen, one participant described her experience with mobile: "I have my phone on me all the time. When I'm asleep it's right there. It's meant to be on-the-go and I'm on-the-go, so I don't have to wait till I get home to get to my desktop."[18] Using a mobile phone to access the Internet and interact with the rest of the world has become the new normal.

## CONVERSATIONAL

As noted earlier, "conversational" is the style of online interaction, meaning short form, back-and-forth, and personable.

Take your own e-mail, for example. When e-mail first became popular for business and marketing, it was common to receive a text-heavy e-mail with several paragraphs of information. Now, companies notify their followers through quick updates; they take heed of the comments that their fans post in the same direct way. Former Crowdtap CEO Brandon Evans says consumers

18   AdmitHub Georgia State University Student Focus Group Interview

want conversations, not ads.[19] People never loved the feeling of being "sold" something, but they still needed advertisement information to make a decision. Now, they want to become connected with the brand or organization. They feel strongly that **taking part is a representation of who they are and their values.**

Against this backdrop, Gen Z desires individualized experiences.[20] A Gen Z student interested in product design may not care as much about how many NCAA titles a school has won as she does about what engineering internship opportunities are available. A student aspiring to public service may want to know about volunteer opportunities and activism at a college but not e-mails or mailers focused on the arts department. Information must be **customized to students' interests** or you risk disengaging them.

The interaction must be personable as well. This goes beyond more traditional understanding of customer service in which being polite and friendly was key. It's important to have a conversation in their terms. This doesn't mean using slang to seem hip or relatable.

---

19   https://www.fastcompany.com/3007362/
     customers-dont-want-ads-they-want-conversation

20   https://www.youtube.com/watch?v=u3DHMlE9LWk

Rather, it means building a conversation on their level and being careful not to alienate them when they ask or say something you don't understand. For example, many Gen Z students use emoji when they have a conversation. To reach Gen Z, you don't have to add emoji to every message—or even understand what every single symbol means—but the use of a smiling face every once in a while can soften some of the formality associated with an educator, administrator, or institution. The **conversation itself is multimedia now**, according to Gen Z marketing duo David and Jonah Stillman.[21]

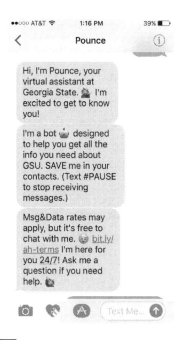

21    https://www.youtube.com/watch?v=Py18PXWJoSY

While not every occasion calls for it, don't shy away from using these personable means of reaching the younger generation. You may miss out on valuable connections by not using them.

**MEET ON MOBILE**

With so much of Gen Z connected through mobile, there has been a paradigm shift in how older generations appeal to their successors. TV ads need to go viral online to carry the greatest impact. Newspaper articles must embed videos that support the focus of the stories. E-mails need vibrant images with robust text and few words. Every brand has to be willing and able to actively engage through conversation.

For Sparks & Honey, a brand is stuck with Millennials if it's not attempting to reach Generation Z by smartphone.[22] In fact, research conducted by Google and YouGov shows that only 9.6 percent of Gen Zers do not use smartphones.[23] Marketing guru Gary Vaynerchuk calls mobile the TV of this generation.[24]

This new generation is like none before. That means

---

22  https://www.slideshare.net/sparksandhoney/generation-z-final-june-17/

23  https://storage.googleapis.com/think/docs/its-lit.pdf

24  https://www.garyvaynerchuk.com/marketing-in-the-year-2016

colleges will need to approach it in new and different ways if they want to fulfill their admission and enrollment goals—and if they want to make powerful and effective connections to Gen Z.

# COMMUNICATION METHODS THAT WORK

**KEY TAKEAWAYS**

- Traditional methods of communication, such as e-mail and even social networks, no longer provide results.
- Text messaging is the most immediate channel for this generation and the simplest way to nudge a student in the right direction.
- Nudges have proven effective in changing student behavior.
- Messages should be easy, attractive, social, timely, and personalized for maximum engagement.

We've discussed the communication channels utilized by colleges and insights about the newest cohort of students, Generation Z. How does this knowledge intersect to help colleges make meaningful connections with prospective students?

## TARGETED

Colleges and universities often purchase student information based on demographic data and academic criteria, but it's understood that not all those students may be interested in receiving information. The critical aim is to target communication to those students who *are* interested in the institution.

There are many ways to establish and deepen communication with potential students. To identify students likely to go through the admission process with your school, for example, allow an additional opportunity to opt-in. As noted in chapter 1, mass e-mails, sandwiched between personal ones, are ignored or merely skimmed. Authorization forms that are distributed at information sessions, during campus visits, via e-mails, or at orientations are a good way to request and document opt-in authorization.[25]

---

25  http://www.nacada.ksu.edu/Resources/Academic-Advising-Today/View-Articles/Advising-plus-Texting-equals-Success.aspx

Be aware: when communicating with students, you must ensure you're doing so in accordance with the Telephone Consumer Protection Act (TCPA). In chapter 5, we discuss in more detail the legalities of messaging.

## CUSTOMIZED AND PERSONALIZED

Electronic communications are imperative in the recruitment of potential students, but impersonal e-mail blasts with general information about an institution don't carry the impact one might assume. Today's students are not captivated by e-mail messaging. Bob Bardwell at Monson Innovation High School says his students generally have their e-mail accounts set up, but they "usually do not check it frequently and never use it."

| | |
|---|---|
| **Oberlin College** | 8:15 am |
| Oberlin says, "You Rock!" | |
| ARTS & SCIENCES ADMISSIONS Hi Anna... | |
| **University of Sioux Falls** | 7:50 am |
| I need to know today | |
| Dear Anna, If you plan to request Best Foo... | |
| **Washington and Lee Unive.** | 7:41 am |
| Could be the last chance for selected st... | |
| Dear Anna, Demystifying the College Inter... | |
| **Case Western Reserve Uni.** | 7:40 am |
| I'm still interested | |
| Dear Anna, I was hoping to have already r... | |
| **Bryn Mawr College** | 7:34 am |

If they want to communicate with someone, it is generally through text messages. Bardwell's students will use e-mail "when absolutely necessary but generally resist."

Most strikingly, if these students receive multiple e-mails from the same institution, "it is often the end of their interest." Bardwell likens it to receiving multiple brochures and mailers from the same college. "One is enough, and sometimes that is one too many" for some students, he says.

Students learn to tune out the noise of mass communication. For them, the noise includes contact that doesn't appear personalized. Fumio Sugihara, director of admissions at Bennington College, addresses the challenge this creates in communicating with Gen Z:

> *"Students are inundated with information, ... so they're fairly adept at sorting through what they do and don't want to engage."*

A recently enrolled student at Georgia State University explained this in a focus group: "I always like it personalized. Not like these messages where a teacher will send something to everybody and it applies to only certain people." As she progressed through the enrollment process, she received helpful text message reminders related to steps on her enrollment checklist. She added, "This is for my FAFSA [Free Application for Federal Student Aid]. 'You haven't completed this portion of FAFSA,' and I was probably the only person who got that."[26]

Receiving relevant information builds credibility with students and makes them value the college as a trusted resource. That can go a long way in building a lasting relationship.

## NUDGES

For decades, colleges and businesses alike have used e-mail as the primary method of communication. More recently, that communication has seen diminishing returns. E-mail open rates and reply rates have waned in effectiveness, and fewer students are answering calls or returning voice mails. Colleges that leverage social networking to share content with students find this channel is also losing popularity among Gen Z. Acknowledging that they must meet Gen Z on the platform it uses, many educators have turned to messaging to reach prospective or current students.

26  AdmitHub Georgia State University Student Focus Group Interview

In the article "Small Nudges Can Improve How Students Apply to College,"[27] Dr. Lindsay Page discusses how text messaging can be a cost-effective way to help students matriculate. She offers three actions based on the findings of her research:

1. Educators need to shift from thinking about whether students apply to college to concentrating on how students navigate the college search and application process.

2. Beyond addressing the application process broadly, educators must focus on understanding the large set of procedural microbarriers involved.

3. Strategies to cultivate student success should include proactive outreach, encouragement, and support.

This ties in with what behavioral researchers Richard

---

27  https://hbr.org/2016/11/small-nudges-can-improve-how-students-apply-to-college

Thaler (University of Chicago) and Cass Sunstein (Harvard Law School) discuss when they underscore the importance of nudges and choice architecture.[28]

**nudge** *verb*

*To give (someone) a gentle reminder or encouragement*

Each year, students go through the processes of applying to college, applying for financial aid, registering for classes, and multiple other tasks. Thaler and Sunstein found that the way these tasks are presented to students can dramatically affect their completion rates. The most successful outcomes are driven by administrators nudging and creating paths of least resistance for college-bound students. Indeed, nudging can boost student success not just on the path to enrollment but also through college.

This insight was echoed in a focus group reacting to AdmitHub's virtual assistant, Pounce, which was created in partnership with Georgia State University to support students through the enrollment process. As one student explained, "I need to be reminded of things, so I liked it,

28  https://ethicslab.georgetown.edu/studio/wordpress/wp-content/uploads/2015/02/ Richard_H._Thaler_Cass_R._Sunstein_Nudge_Impro_BookFi.org_.pdf

and it's like a little mentor saying, 'Oh, make sure you do this. This is the deadline. Get it done.'"[29]

To encourage a behavior, as with a nudge, the Behavioural Insights Team[30] devised the EAST framework.

Messages should be **Easy, Attractive, Social, and Timely.** When nudging a student to complete a certain task, the message should be simple and clear, should capture his or her attention and make him or her want to act, should draw on the supportive power of social networks, and should be sent when the student is in most need of the information. From our own experience, we'd also add **Personalized** to this list—messages should be crafted to each particular student's needs, instead of generically blasted to a mass audience.

## MESSAGING THROUGH TEXT AND CHAT

It is not enough to know that the method of communication that resonates most with Generation Z is **messaging via text message or chat**. You must also know how to structure the information you send via that channel.

---

29  AdmitHub Georgia State University Student Focus Group Interview

30  http://www.behaviouralinsights.co.uk/wp-content/uploads/2015/07/BIT-Publication-EAST_FA_WEB.pdf

In a focus group, recently admitted college students were asked about their texting habits. Their responses included "Every day," "Every day, all day," "A lot," "All day at home," and "At least once a day." While there's a slight variation, they skew toward one end of the spectrum.[31]

As you consider text messaging prospective students, there are best practices shown to bring optimal results, ensuring a positive, efficient experience for everyone involved.

### TEXT MESSAGING BEST PRACTICES

- Introduce yourself in the initial message.
- Make sure you have a clear way for students to opt out of messaging.
- Follow legal texting guidelines (see chapter 5).
- Devise a communication plan for outgoing texts that is proactive and relevant for each student.
- Respond to messages quickly. Less than two hours is ideal. More than two days creates a poor experience.
- Be short and concise with messaging.
- Make the texting more fun and personable. Use GIFs and emoji 😎.

Messaging isn't limited to text and MMS. It's possible to reach students on various platforms. Facebook has

---

31  AdmitHub Georgia State University Student Focus Group Interview

doubled down on its messaging capabilities, and schools should be paying close attention. Smartphone users access Facebook an average of fourteen times per day and spend a daily total of thirty-two minutes on it.[32]

According to Mary Meeker's 2016 Internet trends report, there are more than nine hundred million active monthly users, making Facebook Messenger the second most popular messaging app behind WhatsApp (which has one billion users).[33]

Schools should be looking to engage in conversations with Millennials and Gen Zers—the core demographic of college students who are most active on social platforms. If you have been paying close attention lately, Facebook has released a number of features that give its pages a new suite of tools to engage followers.

## SIX WAYS COLLEGES AND UNIVERSITIES CAN LEVERAGE FACEBOOK MESSENGER

**1. Take advantage of Messenger links and codes.** Facebook recently added links and codes, and colleges can use these to make it fast and easy for people to begin

---

32  http://www.nbcnews.com/technology/
    smartphone-users-check-facebook-14-times-day-study-says-1C9125315

33  http://www.kpcb.com/internet-trends

messaging with them. These short links (m.me/school) open up a conversation with the relevant page in Messenger. Even better, Facebook also has picture codes that can be scanned in Facebook Messenger to begin a private conversation. You can try it out with AdmitHub's page by going into your Messenger app, pressing the People tab, and then scanning the Messenger code, which looks like a profile picture.

This is a game changer when it comes to making traditional methods of outreach more effective. For instance, a college could send out a mailer to prospective students with a link or a picture code to the college's Facebook Messenger page. Students are far more likely to reply in Messenger than they are to send an e-mail or call to sign up or ask questions.

Colleges can encourage their students to save the image code to their photo library, so they can pull up the image and communicate whenever they need assistance.

**2. Update your page's username.** Facebook pages now have the option to choose a username, similar to a Twitter handle. This doesn't have too much functionality yet, but it helps your school become more searchable, making it easier for students to locate your page. Be sure to grab the username you want before someone else does. Facebook could be rolling out more functionality with usernames in the future, but it is a good idea to think of a username now that you'll be happy with long term.

**3. Add private messages to a page from local awareness ads.** Colleges that use local awareness ads can now add a "Send Message" call to action. If a certain post catches someone's eye, they can now message directly from the ad to the page owner. The incoming messages will have an attachment of the ad that prompted the viewer to reach out, giving context for the person responding.

**4. Show a Messenger greeting.** Facebook now allows pages to customize a Messenger greeting. If someone clicks a "Send Message" call to action, he/she will be brought into Messenger and welcomed by a greeting. These greetings are customizable based on the person's

Facebook profile. For instance, a college could say, "Hi, Kirk! Thanks for getting in touch with us on Messenger. Please send us any questions you may have about Owl University." These welcome messages lend a nice, personal touch and prompt the student to start a conversation.

**5. Respond faster by automating answers to FAQs.** All this sounds well and good, **but how can you possibly reply to all these messages**? Facebook has rolled out a "Save Replies" feature that helps administrators respond quickly to a high volume of frequently asked questions. If it typically takes your team a few hours to reply to messages, you should set up an automatic reply telling students they can expect to wait about that long. If you respond to 90 percent of messages within fifteen minutes, you'll earn a very responsive badge (pictured below).

These badges stand out on your page. Your followers will be more likely to reach out when they know they'll get a quick response.

**6. Build a chatbot to facilitate on-demand, two-way conversation.** Another option for replying to messages is by using a chatbot. Facebook announced in April that Messenger now supports chatbots. Instead of a person responding to every message, a chatbot can handle FAQs instantly. Through supervised machine learning, chatbots get smarter and learn to reply to more and more messages over time. When colleges can instantly respond to prospective students, current students, alumni, parents, and fans of the school, the opportunities are endless.

Colleges can build all these strategies, tips, and tools into their enrollment and admission communications plans to spark the best outcomes for their incoming students and their institutions. On the fast-changing technology landscape, keeping up with innovations can be the differentiator among colleges.

# MESSAGING IN THE STUDENT LIFE CYCLE

**KEY TAKEAWAYS**

- Students welcome timely and relevant communication at key points in the enrollment cycle.
- Rapid response times to students' text messages are crucial to building strong connections.
- Artificial intelligence can be an enrollment team's best friend, handling the majority of repetitive Q&A so team members can focus on the students who need the most support.

It's a revolutionary trend that has no end in sight. Gen Z thrives on technology, and its preferred platform for communicating is now also the best tool for keeping young people on track with their college plans. When you want your message seen, you must meet Gen Zers on their own turf: **on mobile.**

Students are welcoming conversation and support throughout the entire enrollment life cycle, and mobile messaging's high engagement rates make it an excellent way to communicate and capture students' attention. When launching a conversation and providing personalized support, it's essential to be relevant and timely. The conversations will change throughout the enrollment life cycle, but the overarching philosophy of providing the right information at the right time holds constant.

### RECRUITMENT

Colleges across the nation have ramped up efforts to attract more—and "better"—prospective students, not only in terms of absolute numbers but also with an eye toward increasing academic quality and diversity (i.e., racial/ethnic, geographic, and socioeconomic considerations, as well as academic interest and extracurricular talent). The types of students that colleges recruit vary by institution, but every vice-president of enrollment and dean of admission still focus on how to fill their applicant pool with qualified students each year.

Public institutions may seek high-achieving, in-state students, enticing exceptional out-of-state and international students, and increasing socioeconomic, racial, and ethnic diversity in their applicant pools. To achieve these recruitment goals, it's important to cast a wide net to prospective students, but only if you can continue to be **responsive**. Impersonal communication blasts typically do not foster the type of relationship building that appeals to prospective students as they search for the college of their dreams.

It's a missed opportunity when a student sends a text message, then has to wait several days to get a simple generic reply. A door gets closed—a door that would have remained open with an immediate and personalized response. Messaging meets Gen Z's criteria: it's conversational and connects with students where they're already talking with friends and family. However, institutions only earn a benefit when they are responsive and personal.

Choosing a college is a major decision for a young person, so naturally, we've seen very high engagement rates when conversationally asking about a prospective student's college plans, instead of blasting the student with a generic reminder about an app deadline, for example. **The conversation is the primary influence site** and where mindsets are formed and changed. It is, once a relationship has been built, also the effective place to nudge students about applying.

*"We were not just looking for a one-way conversation with a student; we wanted ways that we could more personalize that particular process through two-way conversation."*

—SCOTT BURKE, ASSOCIATE VICE-PRESIDENT
AND DIRECTOR OF UNDERGRADUATE
ADMISSION, GEORGIA STATE UNIVERSITY

We've seen many instances in text message conversations where Gen Z students are enthusiastic about a particular institution; at that point, it's best to instantly reply with the information they need.[34] For example, Allegheny College saw an immediate spike in its Facebook group membership after sending a timely message via Chompers, the school's virtual admission assistant. Interestingly, after texting students about an upcoming program, *the college surpassed the total number of evaluations submitted for the previous two events combined.* (See the case study of Allegheny College at the end of the book for more details.)

There are many other key touch points along the enrollment process. Getting students to complete their

---

34  https://www.nytimes.com/2015/09/20/fashion/move-over-millennials-here-comes-generation-z.html

applications is another of them. Colleges traditionally send e-mails and call students on the phone to encourage this step, but these efforts are frequently ignored. A personalized text message, however, informing students **of their own unique steps for completing their applications** can pay big dividends. Not only does it capture their attention, but it can also guide them to follow through on clicking Submit.

After students apply, they inevitably want to know what's up next. They also start asking about the college and its culture. The range of topics is immense, with everything from "When will I get my decision?" to "Tell me more about your engineering program" to "Can I bring my salamander to my dorm room?" Engaging students in these conversations over text message fosters a strong connection to the college and, ultimately, increases the likelihood of attending if accepted. These types of Q&A are perfectly suited to conversational artificial intelligence (AI),[35] which affords instant responses to the inquiring students and saves admission officers hours of precious time.

**YIELD**

For many admission teams, yielding students is top of

---

35  https://campustechnology.com/articles/2017/03/07/using-ai-chatbots-to-freeze-summer-melt-in-higher-ed.aspx

mind and the most important part of the enrollment cycle. Some students can be difficult to reach, making it hard to get an understanding of their college plans. It can also be a challenge to get students to complete important items on the enrollment checklist, among them registering for orientation, submitting tuition deposits, and sending in final transcripts or immunization forms.

Before National College Decision Day on May 1, institutions can utilize texting to gauge interest and help committed students get a head start on their enrollment checklist. Connecting with students during this critical time using more traditional methods of outreach can lead to mixed results because students rarely answer incoming phone calls from numbers they don't recognize, and e-mail open rates in higher education[36] hover in the mid- to lower 20 percent range.

A popular texting intervention to determine yield is a survey in the late-March to early-April time frame to gauge how interested a student is in attending, on a scale of 1 to 4. Based on the reply, admission teams can send a targeted message or encourage further follow-up. If a student replies with a "1" (I'm definitely coming), you can instantly nudge the student to submit his or her intent to enroll. If the reply is a "3" (I'll likely go elsewhere), it's

36  https://mailchimp.com/resources/research/email-marketing-benchmarks/

valuable for the university and admission team to follow up to find out the reason. For those students who reply with a "2," meaning they're on the fence, an admission team can reach out individually and focus on supporting the students in the remaining weeks before decision day.

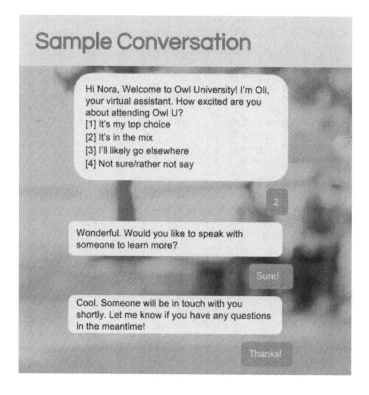

## Sample Conversation

Hi Nora, Welcome to Owl University! I'm Oli, your virtual assistant. How excited are you about attending Owl U?
[1] It's my top choice
[2] It's in the mix
[3] I'll likely go elsewhere
[4] Not sure/rather not say

2

Wonderful. Would you like to speak with someone to learn more?

Sure!

Cool. Someone will be in touch with you shortly. Let me know if you have any questions in the meantime!

Thanks!

Counselors can use the messaging conversation to set up a call to address a respondent's concerns. This not only shows the student that the college cares and wants to help him or her through this process, but it also provides admissions counselors with feedback on how they can impact yield.

Mobile messaging is a great way to send proactive reminders to students who have yet to complete an important task. In a randomized control trial with Georgia State University,[37] we saw that text messaging powered by AI had a positive impact on key items on the enrollment checklist and ultimately increased enrollment by 3.9 percent. (See our case study with Georgia State University at the end of the book.)

## STUDENT SUCCESS AND RETENTION

Student success and retention don't follow quite the same linear path as recruitment and enrollment. However, the same rule applies: being helpful and responsive are of the utmost importance. Students find that being introduced to the resources such as tutoring or having an academic adviser available to them on campus is helpful.

Reminders about financing education carry high value. Many students who previously applied for the FAFSA either forget to or don't realize they have to reapply. Sheila Bair, president of Washington College, notes that one of

---

37 http://blog.admithub.com/
case-study-how-admithub-is-freezing-summer-melt-at-georgia-state-university

the two main reasons students drop out after their first year is financial need.[38] Proactive reminders and guidance for completing the FAFSA or applying for scholarships can push up retention rates.

Colleges should also have a communication flow to address students who are considered at risk.[39] By personally connecting with them before their challenges are exacerbated, colleges can dramatically improve these students' chances for success. Touch point messages such as birthday wishes and congratulations at the finish of the first semester are nice reminders that the institution cares about vulnerable students.

The type of outreach will differ at each institution. As a general rule of thumb, however, educators and administrators should continue to think about how students go from point A to point B in each area of the enrollment life cycle. The goal is to make that journey as seamless as possible, being mindful that Gen Z likes its guidance and support to be **conversational, personalized, and on demand.**

38  http://fortune.com/2016/03/08/mount-st-marys-firing-simon-newman/

39  http://blog.admithub.com/
    different-strategies-for-texting-with-students-through-the-student-lifecycle

# MAKING MESSAGING FEASIBLE

**KEY TAKEAWAYS**

- The average reply rate for text messaging is 40 percent, so it's important that your staff is able to respond in a timely manner.
- Messaging apps that are conversational in nature, such as Messenger and Snapchat, dominate the app market.
- Chatbots are poised to take over apps in terms of engagement because they are simple and easy to use and present zero friction.
- Chatbots can use entire databases of information to personalize conversations to suit your needs.
- When messaging students, it's important to follow the legal guidelines.

As we've discussed, of all the methods of communication sent to students, colleges see the highest response rate via mobile messaging. The strong reply rate for text messaging—an average of 40 percent[40] of messages spark a response—requires that admission staff be at the ready and equipped to handle responses in an efficient and timely manner.

To give you an idea of the staff time needed to respond to messages, the following provides an example of the volume required over the course of a yield season. (The numbers of students and messages are taken directly from our case study with Georgia State University.)

---

40  https://martech.zone/text-messaging/

# 138 DAYS
(INCLUDING WEEKENDS)

## 3,200    SEND    50,000

FIRST-YEAR STUDENTS        INCOMING MESSAGES

IF YOU CAN HIRE A SUPERHUMAN IT WOULD TAKE...

## 30 = 417

seconds per          hours of responding
message              to messages

IT AMOUNTS ALMOST TO

# 52 DAYS

...in the time that staff is also doing everything from hosting yield events to attending spring college fairs and programs, as well as hiring staff, taking much needed vacation, interviewing students, and preparing for the upcoming fall recruitment season.

**AND THEY ARE NOT SUPERHUMANS...**

As noted in chapter 2, Generation Z isn't fond of waiting. Participants in a focus group of first-year students were asked if any aspects of their application and admissions process were especially frustrating. One male participant said, "Humans can be useful, too, if they reply within the time that you want them to reply. I understand that they get a large volume of e-mails every day, but if I could have a timely answer, that would be great."[41] A female participant had a particularly challenging time getting

---

41   AdmitHub Georgia State University Student Focus Group Interview

someone on the phone to answer a basic question. "I called the office of financial aid. I had a scholarship, like a check, I had to send to the school. The first thing, online there was no [address] to send it, so I called and called for two weeks. I got put on hold every single day for an hour. I would just set my phone on my bed and they never answered."[42]

These students were persistent enough to find answers and eventually enroll, but not all are. Consider being in their shoes, or think back to when you've been in a similar situation. Calling customer support and being on hold long enough to memorize the automated message or lyrics to a song is enough to make anyone take their business elsewhere.

### APPS CEDE TO CHATBOTS

Does your school have an app to help students with the admissions process? If so, consider this: How many apps do you have on your phone? Now, how many of them did you use in the last day or two?

For most people with a smartphone, the answer is the same: they use only three apps on a daily basis. A recent

---

42   AdmitHub Georgia State University Student Focus Group Interview

study by comScore[43] breaks down the time spent on those most frequently used apps:

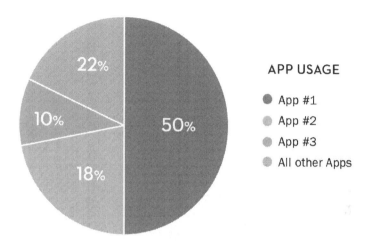

APP USAGE

- App #1
- App #2
- App #3
- All other Apps

This brings the time spent on the most visited three apps to around 80 percent of total app time. Does this sound familiar to your own experience?

Here's another staggering statistic: there are more than 4.2 million apps available for Android and Apple users, yet 40 percent of the most used apps are already preinstalled.

Moreover, *Business Insider* cited a report from tech company Quantcast stating that only **one-tenth of 1 percent** of all apps ever reach fifty thousand users.[44] And get this:

---

43  http://www.comscore.com/Insights/Presentations-and-Whitepapers/2015/
   The-2015-US-Mobile-App-Report

44  http://www.businessinsider.com/app-usage-numbers-quantcast-2014-5

more than 60 percent of all available apps in the App Store have never been downloaded.

The most popular apps dominate because they are on the most downloaded chart. They spread fast when people mention to friends that "you have to check out this new app." There is an app breakthrough barrier that is getting harder to crack, especially for apps serving a relatively small group of people. A university mobile app falls in this category. The top three most downloaded apps in the first half of 2016[45] were Messenger, Snapchat, and Facebook, which are all conversational in nature.

While it's difficult to get people to even download an app, it's even harder to get them to keep using an app. Check out these stats from a recent Localytics post:[46]

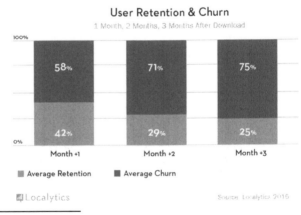

### User Retention & Churn
1 Month, 2 Months, 3 Months After Download

| | | |
|---|---|---|
| 58% | 71% | 75% |
| 42% | 29% | 25% |
| Month +1 | Month +2 | Month +3 |

■ Average Retention    ■ Average Churn

Localytics                              Source: Localytics 2016

45  https://www.surveymonkey.com/business/intelligence/most-popular-apps-2016/

46  http://info.localytics.com/blog/mobile-apps-whats-a-good-retention-rate

Retention here is defined as returning to the app at least once within thirty days. Localytics found app retention after ninety days typically is around 25 percent. So, within just a few months, most apps are losing 75 percent of their users.

Taking this into account, chatbots are a better way to get the attention of students. Chatbots are simple, easy to use, and present zero friction. They exist on the channels that people are most familiar with, such as Messenger, Twitter, SMS text message, and Kik, and they are expanding onto other messaging applications. Unlike apps, bots don't take up space, users don't have to take time to get familiar with a new user interface, and bots will give you an instant reply.

The biggest difference with chatbots compared to apps and websites is that they use language as the main interface. Websites and apps have to be searched and clicked, while bots and people use language, the most natural interface, to communicate and inform.

Historically, apps may have been the en vogue way to engage on mobile, but the data show that most of us use few apps on a daily basis and most apps are hardly touched (if even downloaded at all).

## CHATBOTS

So what is a chatbot and how can it help your staff reach Generation Z?

If you're not certain, you're not alone. Only 22 percent of adults in the United States have heard of a chatbot, according to Publicis Groupe's DigitasLBi November 2016.[47] Like Athena emerging directly from Zeus's head, the first chatbot, named ELIZA, was born from the mind of Joseph Weizenbaum in 1966. This bot and its earliest descendants were simple yet effective. They recognized specific language patterns and replied with evocative canned responses. For example, a user might mention the word *mother*, and the bot might reply with "Tell me more about your family."

Perhaps the most widely used bot in history—AOL Instant Messenger's SmarterChild,[48] which reached more than thirty million people—was also of the pattern-matching variety. Nonetheless, it was entertaining and attracted many millions of users trying to test its limits.

Chatbots can use entire databases of information to personalize conversations to suit your needs. If you're a

---

47  https://www.mediapost.com/publications/article/290971/whats-a-chatbot-most-americans-dont-know.html

48  https://en.wikipedia.org/wiki/SmarterChild

university using a student information system or customer relationship management, all of that data can be used to provide contextualized information to each student and do it in an engaging, conversational, and immediate manner.

Here's an example:

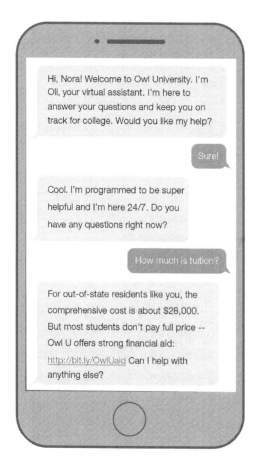

In this case, the bot already knows that the student is from out of state, so it responds with the appropriate answer. The student never had to spend time searching the web to find out what she needed to know. The bot gave her the proper information within seconds.

There are currently ten thousand bots (and counting) on Facebook to help with everything from buying flowers to booking travel. Lately, there has been a series of technological developments coalescing to make it faster and easier to build a chatbot powered by AI.

Chatbots are fast becoming more helpful and more used than apps. They can't answer every question and aren't perfect right now, but they soon will dominate their predecessors for their ease of use and personalized user experiences. Millennials and Gen Zers, in particular, are leading this momentous shift.

## LEGALITY OF MESSAGING

While colleges can now turn to conversational AI to supercharge their staff and amplify their outreach and support, it's important to understand how texting and privacy laws and consumer protection regulations relate to schools' efforts to properly and effectively text students.[49]

---

49 **Disclaimer:** Because legalities of texting are nuanced and can vary by jurisdiction, we recommend consulting your own legal counsel.

There are key differences among various schools: whether they're nonprofit or for profit, how and when they're engaging with students, and the intent and nature of the messages they're sending. But all colleges and universities should be aware of a few laws pertaining to texting prospective and current students and their families.

## TELEPHONE CONSUMER PROTECTION ACT

One of the most important acts to abide by is the Telephone Consumer Protection Act (TCPA),[50] which limits the way prerecorded voice messages, SMS text messages, and automatic dialing systems can be used, and you must comply with its restrictions. The TCPA was passed by Congress in 1991 to stop telemarketers from sending out unwanted messages to millions of people without any way for consumers to opt out of these messages. At a high level, the TCPA prohibits telemarketers from calling or texting without prior express consent when using an autodialer or mass calling/texting system. The three main parts of the TCPA are Do-Not-Call Restrictions, Limitations on Prerecorded Calls, and Limitations on Calls and Texts to Mobile Phones Using an Autodialer.

The twist for many colleges is that tax-exempt, nonprofit organizations are not subject to some provisions of the

---

50  https://transition.fcc.gov/cgb/policy/TCPA-Rules.pdf

TCPA. Colleges that send out informational and educational information are well within the bounds of allowable territory. Nonprofits in general are not held to as high of a standard as commercial organizations in terms of getting consent before calling or messaging. Nonprofits must have oral consent or express consent. For nonprofit colleges, this could come from the Common Application or via an opt-in box on a web form or inquiry card.

If a student provides a cell phone number, colleges are free to assume consent. (We also recommend confirming consent via an initial text message, but there's more on that below.)

In August 2016, the Federal Communications Commission cleared up some gray areas in the TCPA, determining that people who provide their mobile number to a school have provided their prior express consent to receive communications related to the school's core functions. The caveat is that communications regarding non-school-related information is likely not exempt, but again, that shouldn't be an issue for many colleges so long as they steer clear of commercial content unrelated to educational or institutional matters.

In short, the National Association for College Admission Counseling (NACAC) has said that "non-profit colleges and universities should not be concerned about compliance with this law,"[51] but NACAC does recommend reading up on the TCPA and following it closely.

To summarize some of the best practices for colleges in terms of following the TCPA, we recommend:

- Having students opt into messages with express written consent
- Texting students only about information pertaining to the university and not for commercial reasons
- Giving students an opportunity to immediately and easily opt out of text messages (such as replying "stop" or "unsubscribe")
- Immediately introducing the college's identity and the reason it's reaching out to the student

## FAMILY EDUCATIONAL RIGHTS AND PRIVACY ACT

Another set of protections is the Family Educational Rights and Privacy Act (FERPA), which protects the privacy of student education records. This is especially important when it comes to texting because there is the potential for sensitive information to be transferred. If you are texting your students and/or their families, you must be sure that

---

51   https://www.nacacnet.org/knowledge-center/professional-standards/telephone-consumer-protection-act/

you are texting with a secure, FERPA-compliant system. AdmitHub's proprietary software is FERPA compliant, but texting on one's own personal phone might not be, depending on its security systems.

With regard to FERPA, colleges should also be careful about sending (or soliciting) sensitive information via SMS. That means no social security numbers, sensitive financial information, or student grades. As in health care, you may still send this information via SMS but only if the user has been presented with the risks and has expressly consented.

### SECURITY MEASURES FOR SMS AND MESSAGING

Generally speaking, texting is not the most secure means of communication and can be susceptible to spoofing.[52] Most SMS providers don't have antispoofing protection, but good ones do. Services such as AdmitHub require users to reply with validation codes to prevent unauthorized access from hackers.

And remember, "messaging" goes far beyond texting. In fact, other platforms such as Facebook Messenger support full end-to-end encryption, making them even more secure than SMS or e-mail.

---

52  https://en.wikipedia.org/wiki/SMS_spoofing

By employing technology in smart ways, colleges can improve the effectiveness of communications with students, and just as importantly, they can cost-effectively redirect precious admission and enrollment resources to higher value tasks that are best performed by professional staff.

# ENHANCED WITH ARTIFICIAL INTELLIGENCE

**KEY TAKEAWAYS**

- Artificial intelligence (AI) can be separated into narrow and general categories. In this book, we focus on narrow AI, which is the AI of today that can play games, diagnose some diseases, and even drive a car. Each of those programs is designed to work within a single narrow domain.
- We are systematically embracing technology that augments our unique human abilities.
- In education, an AI virtual assistant can be "hired"

to work in tandem with an educator to dramatically increase efficiency in supporting students at scale.

- A chatbot armed with knowledge base software can dramatically boost an enrollment team's ability to handle the large volume of communications that takes place each day.
- Best of all, the more students engage, the greater the knowledge base grows, and the "smarter" the AI becomes.

If you've ever heard the term *artificial intelligence*, then you've likely had one of these three reactions:

- **Fear:** The spectrum of fear ranges from sci-fi dystopian terror that Hal, Skynet, or the Matrix will take over to general unease that a robot might "take" your job away.
- **Optimism:** This is a spectrum that ranges from eager anticipation of self-driving cars or a virtual assistant even better than Siri or Alexa to the ho-hum convenience that Amazon or Netflix recommendations provide us on a regular basis.
- **Confusion:** This is the most common reaction to the term *AI*, which is misused by most people and misunderstood by even more.

First, let's clarify what we mean by artificial intelligence:

- **Narrow AI:** This is the technology of today that can beat the best humans in games such as chess or Go.[53] The technology of "deep learning" is extraordinary in its ability in a single narrow domain. All you need is a lot of data and a lot of computer processing power. This is the AI of today; its programs are bespoke so they are unable to do anything other than what they were trained to do.

- **General AI:** This is the technology of the future (at least thirty years from now) that can learn just like a human and is capable of conversation and even abstract thought.

When we mention AI in this book, we are referring to only narrow AI. If you want to learn more about general AI, we suggest you read *The AI Revolution: The Road to Superintelligence*[54] by Tim Urban, or listen to *Wired*'s interview "President Barack Obama on the Future of Artificial Intelligence."[55] Mr. Obama understands the subject and lays out the broad strokes very clearly.

## "AUGMENTED INTELLIGENCE" TO HELP HUMANS

One of the first big AI headlines of the 1990s was when

---

53  https://www.wired.com/2016/05/google-alpha-go-ai/

54  http://waitbutwhy.com/2015/01/artificial-intelligence-revolution-1.html

55  https://www.youtube.com/watch?v=72bHop6Alcc

IBM's Deep Blue[56] defeated Garry Kasparov to become the world's greatest chess player. It was a decisive moment in the history of technology. The fascinating part of this breakthrough is what happened next. Instead of fading away into irrelevance or becoming events strictly for Luddites, chess tournaments evolved.

Now, chess tournaments unfold as hybrid contests where every human has an AI adviser. Together, these "cyborg" chessmasters[57] are transcending the abilities that either human or computer could achieve alone, and they are getting better by the day. Instead of entering an age where AI is replacing humans, we are systematically **embracing technology that augments our unique human abilities**.

This takes place beyond chess tournaments, too. Every time you fly in a commercial airplane, an AI program does the bulk of the work. The pilot is there to supervise and assume control if something goes wrong. Because of this human-machine collaboration, flying is far safer than driving.

Speaking of driving, new cars also have all manner of intelligent cruise control and automatic braking to make

56  https://en.wikipedia.org/wiki/Deep_Blue_%28chess_computer%29

57  http://www.bbc.com/future/
story/20151201-the-cyborg-chess-players-that-cant-be-beaten

our lives safer. Taking those innovations one step further, Uber and Tesla are leading the way in building self-driving cars that will dramatically reduce accidents on the road.

Twenty years from now, the next generation of children will learn about twentieth-century automobiles and ask, "Did you drive cars and speed down the highway? Wasn't it scary?"

"Yes," we'll reply, hardly able to remember.

### IMPLEMENTING ARTIFICIAL INTELLIGENCE FOR BUSINESS

Business owners are having a hard time seeing the value AI could bring to their companies right now because they are thinking of AI-powered tech in comparison to other software purchases, when **they really need to approach AI as a new hire.**

In the traditional enterprise software model, once a technology is customized and implemented, its value quickly becomes apparent. It is only **after** implementation that traditional technology decreases in value, as newer technology is developed.

AI flips this model completely. **AI-powered technology is at its *least* valuable the day it is implemented.** The technology becomes ever-more valuable to a business once it has had time to learn and be trained for the business's specific use case.

AI works in a similar way to a new hire. For example, if you're handing off your initial customer service to an AI-powered virtual assistant, it must learn several things in order to contribute meaningfully:

- Whom should it be engaging and whom should it escalate to human support?
- What are the bounds of its acceptable responses?
- At what point is it acceptable to end the conversation?

When Google's AlphaGo beat Lee Sedol, one of the best Go players in the world, it marked a high-water moment for AI. Go, the oldest board game in history, has more possible configurations of pieces than there are atoms in the observable universe. While computers decades ago mastered games such as chess, Go wasn't supposed to be conquered for at least another ten years when AlphaGo won.[58]

That actually maps well to what AI in a business setting looks like. On the day you implement AI, it will be nowhere

58  https://www.technologyreview.com/s/546066/
    googles-ai-masters-the-game-of-go-a-decade-earlier-than-expected/

near where you want it to be. However, as it learns, it will quickly outpace your predictions for its value. Banks and companies in the financial sector made this realization, giving to the rise of the various AI-powered virtual assistant chatbots employed by companies such as Bank of America and MasterCard.[59]

## WHAT CAN AI DO FOR EDUCATORS?

*"If AI can help humans become better chess players, it stands to reason that it can help us become better pilots, better doctors, better judges, better teachers."*

—KEVIN KELLY, COFOUNDER OF
IDEO AND *WIRED* MAGAZINE

Imagine if every admission counselor had his or her own AI assistant able to liberate him or her from the repetitive mental tasks that often keep him or her from doing the meaningful work that adds the most value to students' lives.

Like top chess players today, educators could work in tandem with virtual assistants able to dramatically increase their efficiency.

---

59  https://www.nytimes.com/2016/10/27/business/dealbook/banks-bet-on-the-next-big-thing-financial-chatbots.html

Right now, AI technology can automatically remind students about deadlines, gather important information, and provide more than a thousand answers to tens of thousands of student questions about college, college admissions, and financial aid. Best of all, the technology gets smarter every day as it learns from the counselors it is designed to support.

Many questions that students ask are process or status related and can be answered instantly and automatically using an AI virtual assistant. This not only makes a better experience for students by getting a quick reply to them 24-7, but it also takes the burden off a college's busy staff to answer question after repetitive question, over and over again. Scott Burke, associate vice-president and director of undergraduate admissions at Georgia State University, utilizes AdmitHub's AI virtual assistant, Pounce, to complement his current staff.[60] He lauds that it's able to answer more than 80 percent of students' questions, that it responds to questions in as little as seven seconds, and that it has conversations that rival those of humans. What's more, it handles a level of personalized communication and targeted outreach that otherwise would require Burke to hire ten to fifteen more staff members to accomplish.

Instead of sending and responding to thousands (even

60  https://www.youtube.com/watch?v=YLRxrJ5ZNU4

millions) of messages manually, AdmitHub's AI handles nearly 98 percent of the one-to-one communication. Every message is logged, and all student data are recorded. Best of all, in those moments when a student needs the guidance and expertise from a human, the AI will reach out for help and flag the relevant contact.

## WORKING WITH STAFF AND KNOWLEDGE BASE

It's hard to develop deeper relationships with prospective, current, and former students within higher education's increasingly competitive environment. Few institutions are able to drastically increase their resources, so whether an admission staff is reaching out to prospective students, currently enrolled students, or alumni, enrollment leaders will talk about the importance of efficiency in their outreach.

Enrollment teams can take advantage of advances in AI and messaging technology in order to instantly increase their efficiency. A chatbot armed with knowledge base software can provide a huge boost to a team's ability to handle massive volumes of communications each day. Using AI, the chatbot analyzes the incoming message to find a match in the knowledge base, and then the bot automatically replies with the appropriate response. If the bot doesn't recognize a message or understand how to respond, a human counselor can be alerted to take over the conversation.

For an enrollment team, the implications are profound. No, students won't be chatting with a Siri-sounding robot, and no, chatbots won't be taking over university admission offices, but with an installed knowledge base, chatbots can remove menial and repetitive tasks from the plates of staff. To further increase efficiency, a chatbot can also text a contact to schedule a time to talk with a student caller to increase the college's connect rate.

AI chatbots aren't meant to take the jobs of staff, student workers, or call center representatives. In call centers, for example, the bot's function is to allow agents to focus on giving their own warm, personalized touch when talking to prospective students or alumni. A bot can be witty and helpful, but it can't speak about the actual campus experience for students. Using a knowledge base-powered chatbot as a virtual assistant, staff and student workers no longer have to look at their cheat sheets because they can have deeper, organic conversations with their contacts.

Since the Fair Labor Standards Act (FLSA), which came into effect on December 1, 2016,[61] directors of student engagement centers are asking themselves, "Is my staff

61  https://www.dol.gov/whd/overtime/final2016/

spending its time in the most effective way possible right now?" If your staff is replying to FAQs, rarely connecting with contacts on the phone, or spending a lot of time updating contact information, the answer to that question is most likely "no."

Outside of higher education, Dutch airline KLM[62] provides a great example of how this works. KLM uses a Facebook Messenger bot that mixes in human answers with the bot's automated responses. Working together, the human agents and the bot can engage in hundreds of conversations at once. The bot greatly reduces the total volume of inquiries by successfully handling the most common, repetitive issues, freeing up the human agents to focus on more complicated questions and interactions.

This scenario also applies to educational institutions that send thousands of messages per week. With an ever-growing knowledge base, a call center's chatbot can text or e-mail contacts and answer many of the common questions that come in. In AdmitHub's work with its current partners, nine out of ten incoming messages are handled by the bot, and that ratio is increasing as additional messages continue to strengthen the reach of the knowledge base.[63]

---

62  https://messenger.klm.com/

63  http://blog.admithub.com/
    case-study-how-admithub-is-freezing-summer-melt-at-georgia-state-university

## TECHNOLOGY THAT LEARNS: NATURAL LANGUAGE PROCESSING, MACHINE LEARNING, AND DEEP LEARNING

The AI in AdmitHub's virtual assistants utilize natural language processing and machine learning to quickly learn from each interaction. It's a remarkable process where the AI actually becomes smarter with every incoming student question.

Technological progress in AI, particularly in natural language processing, means that chatbots are much more versatile and "smarter" than ever before. Remember ELIZA from chapter 5? ELIZA's simple ability to rephrase the things it's told and ask questions about them is powered by "pattern matching," which essentially uses keywords in a human's statement to trigger a predetermined response. The purpose of chatbots like ELIZA, and later iterations like ALICE,[64] is basically to keep the conversation going.

Most of the chatbots that currently exist can't deliver the power and flexibility of conversational interaction patterns that effectively engage a person and facilitate a meaningful exchange of information. They fall short of meeting the expectations of someone who is accustomed

---

64  http://alice.pandorabots.com/

to having complex, multilayered conversations with other humans in messaging apps.[65]

These "dumb bots" that are simply powered by tree logic don't push the ability of chatbots. Their simplistic frameworks are used to experiment and scaffold toward a more advanced and integrated future. Fortunately, AI can capture the value that a conversational experience offers and doesn't require building a fully featured chatbot or a stand-alone app.

AI chatbots can utilize conversational interaction patterns to engage a user through a familiar interface, such as a text message, that feels like a natural platform for exchanging information. The bots collect multiple data points from a user in a logical progression and adjust responses intelligently and efficiently. By immediately parsing the collected data, the bots improve their understanding of a person's active intent, needs, and desires. Then the bots can deliver personalized content that has a greater potential to satisfy people's needs and, hopefully, exceed expectations. The seeds of trust and loyalty are planted when a person is able to fulfill his or her needs and recognize a satisfying outcome. In higher education, this creates a stronger bond between students and a prospective college or university.

---

65  https://blog.chatbot.com/
    chatbots-without-the-bot-the-power-of-conversational-interaction-patterns-53c8cb8cf3ae

Today's AI-powered chatbots can go far beyond prepro-
grammed responses. "Machine learning" capabilities
enable a chatbot to evolve in response to previous conversations. In other words, the more you talk to it, the
smarter and more conversant it gets. If a question isn't yet
recognized by the AI and isn't already in the knowledge
base, a human can add the proper response so that when
one of the next students asks that particular question, it
is answered instantly.

## THE ARTIFICIAL INTELLIGENCE ON THE HORIZON

Like raising a child, AI needs time to mature, and its
development will require the concerted effort of an entire
industry to achieve its potential. As Hillary Clinton would
say, "It takes a village."

Particularly in education, AI needs the support and collaboration of counselors, teachers, and administrators
everywhere. The journey will not be fast or without stum-
bles, but the promise of every student enjoying 24-7 access
to the collective wisdom of the world's best educators is
within sight.

Looking at the big picture, admission directors have to leverage their departments' assets. Sometimes people don't want to talk to a caller; they just want to get some specific information quickly and easily. A bot with a knowledge base can handle those questions. Just as texting has emerged quickly in the call center space, knowledge bases and AI chatbots are providing incredible opportunities to better serve callers and staff.

The use of student callers can also provide an admission office with valuable support. The most important quality of student callers is their frontline perspective and ability to connect deeply with prospective students or with alumni. When people want to talk to a student, their engagement will quickly bubble to the surface. Student callers will spend their time in meaningful conversations with those people who want to connect.

# CONCLUSION

Generation Z is entrenched in technology in ways that are unlike any of its predecessors. This immersion has shaped its members' tastes, practices, expectations, and even the way their brains function. In order for organizations to engage them in a meaningful manner, it's imperative that older generations and traditional institutions such as colleges adapt to meet Gen Z on its grounds, not the other way around.

Our goal as educators is to reach out and provide an opportunity for students to excel and achieve their greatest potential through education. We are part of a momentum to help the next generation meet its academic and career aspirations. It's at the heart of what motivated us to join the profession. Even while drudging through everyday bureaucracy and trying to keep pace with an ever-changing technological culture, we can achieve this goal.

Colleges and universities are now working with a generation unlike any other. At the same time, institutions have heightened their commitment to build community beyond just when students enter to study—as alumni, donors, mentors to students, volunteers, and board members. Because the relationship starts with the admission process, it means that effective engagement at that point is crucial. If successful, it lasts not only through the enrollment cycle but throughout a person's entire life.

Our hope is that this book has equipped you with an understanding of Generation Z students and what shapes their culture. As digital natives, they are one of the most mentally agile, informed, and connected groups in America. With smartphones in their hands and a world of information at their fingertips, they are accustomed to personalized, immediate experiences.

With guidance on when and how to connect with them, you can develop strategies on how best to support them in reaching their goals. Because they welcome helpful nudges, it's important to give them the information they need to pursue their aspirations while not undermining their independence. In doing this, they develop strong bonds and a healthy reliance on the wisdom of advisers.

We've provided perspective in how to reach them on a fast-changing communications landscape. We have armed you with the insights and tools you need to leverage cutting-edge technology. We have found that one of the oldest and most persistent mobile technologies, messaging, is welcomed and widely embraced by today's students. So we must meet Gen Zers where they spend their time: the cell phone.

There is tremendous opportunity in employing messaging to support students on their path to and through college. With advancements in conversational AI, admission and enrollment teams now have the power to efficiently communicate with massive numbers of students, hold personalized conversations that build strong relationships, and significantly boost key enrollment metrics.

By combining text messaging with conversational AI, we can extend the impact of smart communication beyond college admission for our youngest generation. This approach gives us a means of adapting to and aligning with Generation Z's preferences. It opens a channel to continue a conversation that helps the largest population since the baby boomers to make meaningful decisions.

In the context of higher education, it helps colleges and universities build relationships and communities that extend not just for the college years but also for a student's lifetime.

# CASE STUDY #1

## HOW GEORGIA STATE UNIVERSITY SUPPORTS EVERY STUDENT WITH PERSONALIZED TEXT MESSAGING

Last year, Georgia State University (GSU) became the first college in the United States to employ a virtual assistant to support students through the enrollment process. GSU had been struggling with significant and rising summer melt. As traditional methods for reaching students—e-mail, phone, and physical mailings—declined in effectiveness, GSU became aware of research showing that text message nudges could be a remedy.[66] However, the university was unsure how best to implement an intervention to more than seven thousand students without overwhelming

---

66  http://curry.virginia.edu/uploads/resourceLibrary/9_Castleman_SummerTextMessages.pdf

its admissions staff. The prospect of adding thousands of student text messages to the staff's weekly workload seemed daunting.

So, GSU called on AdmitHub to create Pounce, a custom virtual assistant to guide students through enrollment, to answer their questions 24-7, and to build strong personal connections to the university. After a rigorous study led by well-known research scientists Lindsay Page[67] and Hunter Gehlbach,[68] results showed that AdmitHub was responsible for a **21.4 percent decrease in summer melt and a 3.9 percent increase in enrollment.** Overall, GSU reported a record year for enrollment, with much of its success attributable to Pounce, AdmitHub's innovative technology for engaging and supporting students.

### ORIGIN STORY

In late 2015, GSU came to us with a major challenge. The university was grappling with runaway summer melt that had risen from 12 percent to nearly 19 percent in a few short years. Students who "melt," or dropout, disproportionately come from underserved communities, which frequently lack supportive resources to help students navigate challenging financial, academic, and social situations.

---

67  http://www.education.pitt.edu/people/profile.aspx?f=LindsayPage

68  http://education.ucsb.edu/research-faculty/bio?first=Hunter&last=Gehlbach

GSU's reputation for progressive thinking is well documented. It is number one in the Top 5 Most Innovative Universities rankings by *U.S. News & World Report*.[69] Meanwhile, its First-Year Experience program and Freshman Learning Communities are notable examples of how GSU is reputed as a national leader in student support. When it came to summer melt, GSU sought to test and design innovative solutions to this challenge and to serve as a model for student support across higher education.

During conversations, GSU's admission staff agreed that the traditional methods of connecting with students—e-mail, phone calls, and snail mail—just weren't working with Gen Z.

GSU also understood that text messaging is the best way to engage the current generation of students. Previous research on this subject by Page and Ben Castleman[70] showed that even simple text reminders had a meaningful positive impact on student enrollment, offering a scalable, cost-effective approach to addressing summer melt.

Although GSU was well aware that text messaging could help solve its problem, there was worry about the increased workload that extra text message communica-

---

69  https://www.usnews.com/best-colleges/rankings/national-universities/innovative

70  http://curry.virginia.edu/uploads/resourceLibrary/9_Castleman_SummerTextMessages.pdf

tion would place on existing staff. Without the budget to hire additional personnel, the university turned to a more scalable solution from AdmitHub that used cutting-edge artificial intelligence (AI) technology.

## SAY HELLO TO POUNCE

MEET POUNCE

To help scale GSU's personalized student communication, we created Pounce—a custom virtual assistant for the university's admissions. Pounce was designed to help students by sending timely reminders and relevant information about enrollment tasks, collecting key survey data, and instantly answering students' many questions around the clock.

## A RANDOMIZED CONTROLLED TRIAL WITH ADMITHUB

During the summer of 2015, we came across Lindsay

Page's work and were floored by its impact on students' lives. We were fortunate to connect with her then and even more flattered when she expressed excitement over the potential for our technology to positively impact students on a much greater scale. As luck would have it, the GSU admission team was also in the midst of reading Lindsay's book on summer melt and was similarly impressed. Wheels started turning on the possibilities for a collaboration, and a randomized controlled trial (RCT) was born.

An RCT is a major leap of faith for an early-stage start-up, to be sure, but it reflected how deeply we believed in the power of our technology and the mission of our work to support students to and through college. Additionally, given GSU's many new initiatives and its fast-paced innovation, we wanted to ensure we didn't misattribute the results of one change to another.

**RCTs are the gold standard for evaluating program effectiveness** *and are the most reliable way to determine what works and what doesn't.*

With the RCT structure in place—with half of the incoming freshman class chosen at random to use Pounce and the other half selected for the control group—we spent the first few months of 2016 working closely with GSU's admissions and IT teams developing the "brain" of Pounce.

Finally, the day came when we were ready to launch with thousands of students.

## DAY ONE: WILL OUR HEADS EXPLODE?

In early April 2016, we were "first day of school" levels of nervous as we introduced Pounce to GSU's incoming admitted students. Despite our trepidation, Pounce's introduction was a huge success. After switching Pounce on, 3,114 admitted students were texting away, representing a 90 percent opt-in rate among admitted students with valid US cell phone numbers.

## APRIL - AUGUST 2016

**3,114** students　　　**90%** opt-in

While thrilled with the student engagement, we could never have predicted how transformative this platform would be for our admission partners. Working hand in hand with GSU's team, we saw how Pounce supercharged response times and the level of support the admissions team was able to offer. It was like wearing an Ironman suit for communication—a single person could manage literally thousands of conversations simultaneously.

## MESSAGING ACTIVITY

By program's end, 63 percent of all students in the treatment group had engaged with Pounce on at least three separate days during the enrollment process; each had exchanged an average of sixty messages. Of the fifty-thousand-plus student messages received, less than 1 percent required the attention of GSU staff. The rest were handled by Pounce or AdmitHub staff overseeing the virtual assistant's learning process.

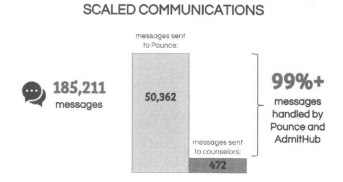

SCALED COMMUNICATIONS

185,211 messages

messages sent to Pounce:

50,362

messages sent to counselors:

472

99%+ messages handled by Pounce and AdmitHub

## HOW WAS POUNCE RECEIVED?

So how do all of these messages translate into student satisfaction and performance? Simply put, students **loved** chatting with Pounce: 80 percent gave it four or five out of five stars, and **94 percent recommended that GSU introduce Pounce to next year's admitted class.**

## STUDENT SATISFACTION

**80%**

gave Pounce
4 or 5 stars

**94%**

recommend GSU
offer Pounce to
next class

Enumerating their favorite characteristics, students noted that they appreciated Pounce's casual language, ease of accessibility, and personalization of messages. One student said, "It was the easiest part of enrollment."

### STUDENT TESTIMONIALS

"I love Pounce. It's not pushy."

"I'd rather get a text than an email."

"I liked how convenient it was. I didn't have to look through my emails, I just went to my text."

"The language doesn't sound like a machine. It's chill."

"I like how it was personalized to me."

In our focus groups with students who engaged with Pounce, we learned why students especially liked the interaction. For starters, they didn't feel judged for asking what might seem like a "stupid" question. They also appreciated the instantaneous responses, especially when they asked questions at all hours of the night, like this:

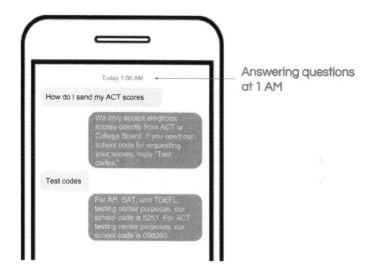

Overall, Pounce made for a pretty great Sherpa for the admissions and enrollment process.

**RESULTS!**

What's truly impressive is that throughout the course of the RCT, the treatment group (those students who texted with Pounce) had significantly higher completion rates of key enrollment steps than the control group. Furthermore, because students communicated their decision changes to Pounce in real time, GSU always had its finger on the pulse on the enrollment intention of students in the treatment group.

Here are the results for the students who committed to GSU in terms of percent impacts:

**+3.3%**
Orientation attendance

**-16.85%**
FAFSA verification

**+14.9%**
Loan counseling

**+3.9%**
Enrolled at GSU

**+12.2%**
Loan acceptance

**+9.3%**
On-time immunization submissions

**+6.25%**
On-time transcript submissions

Overall, for students who committed by June 1—GSU's priority deadline—**the treatment effect was a 3.9 percent increase in enrollment and a 21.4 percent reduction in summer melt.** This is a significant contribution to what turned out to be a record year for enrollment[71] at the university.

As for the results he saw with students, GSU's assistant vice-president for undergraduate admissions, Scott Burke, said:

---

71  http://news.gsu.edu/2016/08/22/
    georgia-state-sets-records-academic-quality-size-first-post-consolidation-freshman-class/

*"[Pounce] has exceeded my wildest expectations. What [AdmitHub is] doing is truly making a difference, and [it] always has the best interest of the student and the institution in mind. I cannot say that about many of the companies that I have done business with in my twenty-plus-year higher education career."*

Following the success of last year's interventions on summer melt, we are excited to expand our partnership with GSU this year. Not only will we be increasing our scope of work with its recruitment and admission efforts, but we will also be working on exciting new initiatives around student success.

To build AI that can understand language is a daunting task, but we are greatly encouraged by the progress our technology has made over the past twelve months, and we're even more impressed with how enthusiastic students were about AdmitHub.

The fact that AdmitHub's Pounce was empirically proven (when compared to a control group) to be a meaningful guide through enrollment lends promise to our technology being applied at scale to benefit students and families across the nation.

# CASE STUDY #2

## ALLEGHENY COLLEGE MAINTAINS A PERSONAL TOUCH WITH TEXT MESSAGE AUTOMATION

There are more than two hundred liberal arts colleges in the United States. These institutions primarily promote small classes, low faculty-to-student ratios, and a high level of personal engagement between students and college staff.

All liberal arts colleges pride themselves on the personal touch in admission and enrollment processes. Admission officers typically manage geographic territories and develop close relationships with the prospective students they meet at high school info sessions, college fairs, joint college travel programs, and campus visits. Many also interview students and serve as the primary contact for them as they go through the application process.

So how does a small liberal arts college use text message automation to be instantaneously available for students of the on-demand generation?

## SUCCESS LEADS TO DIFFERENT KINDS OF CHALLENGES

Consider the case of Allegheny College, one of the Colleges That Change Lives (CTCL).[72] As a CTCL institution, Allegheny is committed to **"building the knowledge, character, and values of young people by introducing them to a personalized and transformative collegiate experience."**[73]

In our conversations with **Cornell LeSane,** vice-president for enrollment and dean of admissions, and **Jason Andracki,** senior assistant director of admissions, we learned that while Allegheny has been fortunate in recent years with record numbers of inquiries and applications, its staff size has remained static.

*"It's been a challenge to provide the type of personal outreach that a student who chooses Allegheny expects,"* said

72  https://ctcl.org/about/

73  https://ctcl.org/about/

Andracki. *"It's hard to juggle all of these prospective students with limited staff time."*

While Allegheny remained intent on providing personalized support to its prospective students, the college has faced several challenges in meeting this goal:

1. Traditional methods of outreach (i.e., e-mail, phone, and snail mail) showed diminishing returns on staff time and investment.

2. The staff was feeling the crunch of putting in additional hours trying to connect with students, which, ironically, left staff with less time for one-on-one student relationships.

3. In alignment with their mission, enrollment professionals were constantly seeking ways to personally engage students in order to increase their reach and improve the quality and diversity of each incoming class.

## MEETING STUDENTS WHERE THEY ARE

As LeSane and Andracki thought of ways to meet these challenges, they looked into one-to-one text messaging. They understood that texting was the best way to capture students' attention, and according to Andracki, "We didn't want to be left behind."

Recent studies[74] have shown that 98 percent of text messages are read within fifteen minutes while only about 20 percent of e-mails are opened. Andracki even mentioned his own personal experience on the matter:

*"I have a lot of unread e-mails in my inbox, but I don't really have unread text messages."*

—JASON ANDRACKI, SENIOR ASSISTANT DIRECTOR OF ADMISSIONS, ALLEGHENY COLLEGE

This isn't to say that LeSane and Andracki didn't have any concerns about texting. For one, they were hesitant to text message students during the recruitment process. They didn't want to pester them if the students weren't truly interested in Allegheny. They were also cautious about messaging costs, although they came to realize that most students now have unlimited texting plans.

Their largest concern was saddling their already-overworked staff with the responsibility of responding to incoming student messages. With the rising number of inquiries and applicants, they wanted a way to meet students where they are, maintain the personal touch crucial to their mission, and prevent burdening their staff with more work.

---

74  http://mobilesquared.co.uk/media/27820/Conversational-Advertising_SinglePoint_2010.pdf

## CHOMPING AT THE BIT

As LeSane and Andracki evaluated text messaging options, they knew they needed a solution that would be responsive to students and capture their attention, while also allowing the technology to work for them, instead of the other way around. "It's not that we don't want to work hard," said Andracki, "but we eventually do sleep at times and we have time outside of the office where we're not tied to our computer and our phones."

They decided to utilize AdmitHub's automation technology to give them the best of both worlds. With that decision, Chompers became a reality. Similar to Georgia State University's Pounce, AdmitHub developed a virtual assistant powered by artificial intelligence for Allegheny College with the persona of the school's beloved alligator mascot.

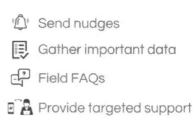

'Send nudges

Gather important data

Field FAQs

Provide targeted support

As it engages students over text message, Chompers does everything from nudging students to complete their applications to reminding them to register for on-campus events. Even better, it answers their every question within seconds, 24-7.

LeSane and Andracki decided to use Chompers throughout the recruitment and enrollment process. By giving students the power to pause the conversation, or even stop it altogether, the Allegheny admission staff is able to better evaluate student interest across its inquiry pool, while alleviating its concerns about annoying students who might not be interested.

> *"To have Chompers there to answer questions from students was really reassuring. It was going to allow us to target outreach to students, and it was better than picking up the phone and cold-calling or sending out an e-mail blast to a thousand students and hoping for 30 percent of them to read it."*
>
> —JASON ANDRACKI, SENIOR ASSISTANT DIRECTOR OF ADMISSIONS, ALLEGHENY COLLEGE

## PROMISING RESULTS

In only the first few months of Chompers text messaging with students, LeSane and Andracki recorded valuable recruitment results in several key areas:

- **The Class of 2021 Facebook page saw 30 new sign-ups** within the first hour of Chompers's message campaign, **and 268 sign-ups (out of 414 students, or more than HALF of the entire group)** since Chompers started messaging. "[The page] wasn't something that we were hiding from them, but it was a new way of communicating with them," Andracki said. "It was a concrete reminder that they're not reading everything in the acceptance letter even though we pore over it. They're not reading every single e-mail that we send, and it's great to see immediate results like that."

- For a recent on-campus program, after Chompers messaged back and forth with attendees, Allegheny saw **more than double the registrations than for the previous two events combined.**

- For on-campus programs, Allegheny is receiving more **student evaluations** via Chompers than ever captured before. "We like to think what we do is really great," said Andracki, "but we need to hear that from our guests to refine and improve our programs, and we've definitely gotten a **much better response in our post-visit survey** with Chompers, particularly from students. In the past, it's been the parents who do those evaluations, and while we want to keep them happy, we also really want to hear from students."

## THE STAFF DIGS CHOMPERS

Aside from the increased metrics and engagement on the student end, it's worth noting that the admission team at Allegheny has already formed a strong positive relationship with the technology. Andracki noted, "They've been very excited about Chompers. For one, it's sharing some of the work."

*"It's almost like a virtual staff member, so we're always happy to have extra help."*

—JASON ANDRACKI, SENIOR ASSISTANT DIRECTOR
OF ADMISSIONS, ALLEGHENY COLLEGE

The admission team is young and mobile-friendly, and its members previously had done some texting with students using their personal cell phones. Andracki said, "Having a way of reaching students via text without [staff] having to do it on their own personal device has been great—and has been a relief for them."

As the Allegheny team continues to work side by side with Chompers, it appreciates that the best way to maximize the technology's capabilities and enhance the personalization of communication with students is to actively participate in the training of Chompers's knowledge base. Andracki humorously (but spot-on) likened Chompers to "a young alligator" and said, "We want to help to feed

Chompers's knowledge, help it grow, learn more about Allegheny. It's also given us an insight into different ways that students respond and ask questions."

## UP NEXT FOR CHOMPERS

With Chompers chatting away with thousands of students interested in Allegheny College, we're looking forward to expanding its role this season to assist admitted students with the enrollment process and, in the future, to help currently enrolled students build stronger connections to their campus community.

# ABOUT THE AUTHORS

 **KIRK DAULERIO** is cofounder and Chief Evangelist at AdmitHub. He previously worked in athletics at his alma mater, Swarthmore College; on the admissions staff of Princeton University, University of Pennsylvania, and Bowdoin College; in college counseling at Gould Academy; and as Director of Member Relations for the Common Application.

**ADRIAN SERNA** is an education management professional who began his career as an instructor at Stanford University, his alma mater. He worked in private education, developing individualized programs for students of all ages and abilities. As Director at Cardinal Education, he managed operations, trained academic coaches, and launched multiple nonprofit initiatives.

Made in the USA
Lexington, KY
16 November 2017